Reality

I0224019

ANDREW ALDRED

chipmunkapublishing
the mental health publisher

Reality

Dedicated "To Jane"

ANDREW ALDRED

The Way of the World

You cannot change the way of the world.
Nobody is satisfied with what they have any more.
Refugees are trying to build a life any way they can.
If they trample all over us, they have had it done to them.
There will always be wars and I have been involved.
You can be fighting to survive wherever you are.
People will always be wanting to take what is rightfully yours
Everybody gets paid and they have to earn the money.
The police are busy trying to do their best for everybody.
And they are only people the same as the rest of us.
I am not a vigilante and I do not carry any weapons.
I am just a time served soldier trying to live out his life.
The world was here before me, and it will be here afterwards.
You cannot change the way of the world.

Abuse

If you want the abuse to stop it will
They always want to make you behave.
But they are in charge, and they want that power.
You have to break free of the chains yourself.
Who you are will always follow you around.
I belong in Bolton, and I will stay there.
We are all fighting to stay above ground.
And we all value our lives and what we have got.
If you misbehave you will always be abused
But sometimes the punishment does not fit the crime.
I have been punished all my life since boyhood.
But I am a peaceful man who is growing old.
If all I can do is be alone that is up to me
I am a fifty-eight-year-old veteran, you see.

End of an Era

I had to finally let Jane go today.
I gave her everything for years.
I worked night and day to make her happy
And now I am worn out and she needs to do it herself.
We have lived in separate houses for a while.
We both need to go back to who we were.
We are both better off and a lot happier.
She has got a family and I have got a brother.
We have been everywhere together and done everything.
It is now time to get on with our separate lives.
We still love each other but the magic has gone.
We have not been able to have sex for ten years.
Everybody else has always got in the way.
She can clean herself up and get back in the field.
I have been loved and need to be alone.
It is the end of an era, and I am so tired.

Coming Out

I am trying to tell you who I am.
I have become my mental illness.
It is the life I have had that has made me ill.
And now it is the only life I have got.
If I tell you about it, you might think I am alright.
I have had every trick pulled and nobody told me.
Everybody wants a piece of me, and I am trying to survive.
You can get killed by a lot of things in life.
I am coming out, but I rarely leave my house these days.

Father

My dad is a little man, but he is fearless.
He has done a lot and lasted for many years.
He used to be in the Navy with special boats.
He joined his family firm and worked for them.
He worked in industry and taught people.
I came back from the army in pieces at twenty.
I did not realise I would always be in
We are all people whatever walk of life.
He taught me to be who I was and took responsibility.
He will always talk to me even now.
He is a good man who tries very hard.

ANDREW ALDRED

Someone I forgot to Be.

I have been out of the army for a long time.
But I have to remind myself who pays me.
And you can bet your life it's a decent wage.
My girlfriend's family does not pay me anything.
She feeds me now and then but that is all.
I am up to my neck in shit at the moment.
Because of the books I have written to get myself better
I have done everything I can for my girlfriends' family.
So, I might as well do something for myself.
I did not ask for a discharge certificate last time.
So, this time I guess I am going to have to do that.
The corporal always said you have Bob Hope and no hope.
Buy I have never been totally defeated.
I have always been able to pick myself up.
I know what goes on round here.
They do not think I can hear what they say.
But I am just getting on with my life.
I probably am the thing that should not be.
But I really do not give a shit anymore.
I have turned full circle into a mental illness.
My girlfriend was the best thing that happened to me.
But nothing good lasts forever
Death comes along or it gets too much.
I am making a new will out to the army.
They are the only ones that ever gave me anything.
I have always been sorting things out for other people.
And now it is time I sorted my own life out.
I will go back to being someone I forgot to be.

The Old Me

You want to turn me back to the old me?
Well, there are still knives in the kitchen drawer.
I still like drinking when I get the chance.
I still like the sound of rock and roll music.
And I would really like anybody to stop by
If I could be bothered to open the door
Nobody gets in unless I know who they are.
I am the old me, but I am a lot better
These days I have learned to take my medication.
I do not have a constant problem with vision.
I am diseased but I am well in other ways.
I have learned to do all sorts of things by myself.
Yes, I am the old me but a lot better.

Conversion Therapy

Well good luck with your conversion therapy
But it has not worked very well so far.
After forty years you have not broken my will
My mother tried with hormones when I was young.
The army tried again but to no avail.
They try to teach me who I am, but they do not know.
They do not realise it is them that are homosexual.
It's like saying I'm not gay but my boyfriend is.
They do not discriminate but you can bet that I do.
I can shag anybody, but I do prefer women.
I do not go hanging around in toilets like George Michael
People in the army are mostly gay arse shaggers.
All they want to do is feel they are in charge of somebody.
The corporal always said I was a sexy beast.
Well, hell, at least he told me so.
The rest of the world just wants to invade me.
Whilst I am asleep and unaware and it's too much
Get on with your own craziness and mental illness.
You know I have never been diagnosed as psychopathic.
But I can bet some of you will be down the line.
We can carry on as before or make a change.
Sex should always be by consent and please note.
My door is always locked, and I am barricaded in.
Will you all please piss off and fuck each other?
I cannot get on with the gay thing because it is not me.

Do My Job

You can step in my shoes and take my pay if you want.
But you are better advised to be yourself.
It certainly is not easy being loved to death.
It might suit some people very well.
But I am sure as hell not one of them.
You can cross examine me all you want.
But I am angry as hell, and I need to tell you that.
You can say worse things happen at sea.
And they probably bloody well do
Spare a thought for somebody who started as a foot soldier.
And as a military policeman before that in the regular army
They did not even give me a proper discharge notice.
I really do not care what happens or where I end up.
Enough is enough and the buck stops here.
If I say I want to be retired it had better happen

The Pen or the Sword

Which is mightier, the pen or the sword?
They are both pretty powerful tools in the right hands.
You can write a thousand books without saying anything.
They will be exactly the same or they will not.
You have to aim for something different.
And then you have to sell your own brand
It is difficult if you are a nobody.
People always need a platform to sell things off.
So, I have built my own out of books.
This is number seventeen and if you want me to stop.
You had better make sure I get paid.
The rest of you might be the power of the sun.
But if I was the moon, I would blot you out.

Drinking Again

I need to flush my system out with alcohol.
I cannot carry on without it.
Everybody that knows is so concerned.
But all they are is a bunch of bloody hypocrites.
If you look in their houses the cans are piled high
Its full of takeaway food and bloody junk
I cannot eat a lot at the moment.
So, I will be my dirty self and have a beer.

Running on Abuse

This country runs on witchcraft and abuse.
We are the same bunch of pagans we always were.
Shout at me all you want, and I will laugh.
You are all a joke, and I am the punchline.
You might think we are all on lockdown.
But life is going on and there is nothing anybody can do.
The world will not reset, and everything is in real time.
We all have our jobs, but we do them how we want.
The employer can always sack you and get someone else.

Give You Everything?

I cannot give you everything for nothing.
I am old and tired, and I need it myself.
I need to put it back where it came from
My money will go back to the army when I am dead.
They are the only people who deserve it.
Everybody gets their fair share in this life.
And that should be all they need to get by
I get a disability pension and a retirement pension.
And I also get independence payment.
Believe you me it has not come for free.
You have got your own money so spend it.
Sometimes people need to look at what they do for me.
And all most of them can do is leave me alone.
We all get paid by the state to take care of things.

ANDREW ALDRED

It Will Work Itself Out

This is a situation which is not of my own choosing.
A gambling man would say I lost years ago.
But I have carried on beating the odds forever.
And I always will because nobody helps me.
I am an independent cell that does as it chooses.
Because the rest of you have enabled me to do this
Well sort it out yourselves and take the glory.
I always wanted to pass the time and listen to music.
Well now I have the choice for the first time.
If you want to be like me carry on misbehaving
Carry on not doing your jobs and saying no to everything.
Make each other and society pay if you have to
Our lips are sealed and so are our documents.
We have all got what we have got, and we deserved it.
I know what happens in these bloody wars, I always have.
Those who want to will fight on and get decorated.
We have all done our job for the King. Long live the King

Too Long in Exile

We can all live in exile if we want.
Look at Prince Harry and look at myself.
Everybody is working for the family firm in some ways.
Sometimes we start our own families.
Sometimes we stand by them and sometimes we do not.
You can be a blood relative of mine if you want.
But it sure as hell would not be advisable.
The money is better off going to the British Army
I have got what I need. My love comes for free.
I will always have enough for the rest of my life
I am who I am and that is all that I can be.
I come from a regiment that does not exist.
We are all on the march of the damned.
You can take part if you want but I do not.
I used to but the best way I can show my respect.
Is to buy a poppy at Asda and stay away.

ANDREW ALDRED

Are You Any Different?

We can be a nation of wallflowers if we want.
Cover ourselves in tattoos, perfume and clothes.
But it is not really very much camouflage.
You want to be an advertisement for yourselves?
You all have too much money and too little sense
Sooner or later we all have to get on with it.
I know the law and they cannot teach me anything.
There is a law for the rich and a law for the poor.
And I am just trying to get on the best way I can.
You will all be hoist by your own petard.
You can go to prison. I will stay at home.
I am in my own cage and at least I can drink.
I do not need company anymore.
Everything I need is here and I do not have to go far.
Throw a boomerang and it will come back to you.

Sacrificed at War

If my sergeant had wanted me to live
The least he could have done was to stand with me.
So, he has been sacrificed and I have not.
But which sergeant am I talking about?
I have been under quite a few. Where are they?
Everybody has gone to seed these days.
We are all doing our own thing and cannot be bothered.
I have fought on for long enough.
I will live on the rest of my life in peace.

Betrayed

The only person you ever betrayed was yourself.
You are always ill and demand much attention.
You are trying to play everyone and think you are clever.
You are chasing money and an independent life.
But it will kill you because your health is not good.
If you want to walk in my shoes, you can babe.
But it's a hell of a difficult road and you have no recourse.
You have nothing to fall back on apart from your mother.
Some people can last alone, and some people cannot.
You always wanted company and a house full of boys.
Well, you can have that babe, but I have gone.
I have seen and heard enough, and I know all your secrets.
You will betray yourself sooner or later babe.
And somebody else can take it in the neck for you.

Locksmiths

If the police ever wandered what they were looking for
It is a set of rapists with every key you could imagine.
They all come from a criminal background.
And they should never have been given a chance in life.
Because they abused the trust they were given
And they have let everybody down in a big way.
I fix my own locks these days because I can.
I would not want one of these men.
They all need locking up as soon as possible.
They can all be traced, and they are on the computer.
The guilty ones can go back to jail for me.
Also, people who keep keys for other people
They all have a hidden agenda and cannot be trusted.
There ought to be an amnesty of keys amongst other things.
If you want to be honest you can do the right thing
People need to keep their own keys and look after them.

Take Your Drugs and Behave

Gangsters will always give you a load of drugs.
They will get you hooked any way they can.
And the medical profession think you work for them as well.
They will make you so stoned you can do nothing.
In order to teach you a lesson and make you respect them
I would have anyway if people had cared about me.
The army said I was a quiet man who kept himself fit.
People try to ruin my health any way they can.
Drugs ought to be provided by the medical profession alone.
A lot of psychiatrists' abuse people with drugs
They confuse issues and refuse to believe you.
Because they have not gone a clue and they do not know any better
If you take drugs, you should get them yourself.
Everyone should take their own drugs and no other peoples.

Ever Fallen in Love

She was the right girl to start with
We have been hammering away at each other for sixteen years.
We started off having wild sex and partying.
We tried marriage and the family thing.
But it has not worked, and she can only be herself.
We are better suited to being apart these days.
But we are both too old to try again.
We have been everywhere and done everything.
And now it is time for us both to be alone.
Yes, we have both been well and properly tangoed.
It has been a hell of an education, and it tore us apart.

Round the Block

I have been moved out of a lot of houses.
All over Bolton and some I even lived in twice.
I cannot make something stick even now.
I have done everything in the house I live in myself.
Or I have paid the fees and let somebody else do it for me.
I have been to the county nick and the local
And regional mental hospitals time and time again
What is the point of all of this I ask of you?
Can you not just let me be or do I have to do everything twice?
Everyone always wants to teach me a lesson and there is always
something.
I have been in love, and I do not want to go there again.
I cared about my family and that of my girlfriend.
People continually let me down, but I am still alive.
I have done everything at least once. Leave me alone.

Second Best

I have the second best of everything.
It is all I ever wanted.
It does not take too much to make me happy.
If anybody wants to stop by
I will be very glad to see them.
Just knock on my door
And if I am in and decent it will be opened
I have very little of everything
I have a house and a car.
And my house is full of things.
That are all outdated and second-hand.

Just Mentally Ill

I am just a mentally ill ex-soldier.
My books tell a tale of things.
Everybody thinks what is right for them.
I am too old to be a screaming madman.
Or a knife wielding maniac any more
So, I have written a few books for you.
And used poetic license with some things.
Eventually you will let me get on.
I have enough for myself and no more
I have already paid for my crimes.
Leave me alone is the least anyone can do.

Salvation

My books are my salvation.
My record of everything I have done.
They keep me occupied.
But sooner or later there is no more.
I am not an SAS man.
I am just an ex-soldier.
I went through the Paras.
I passed P company at a young age.
I have been to prison.
I have been to mental hospital.
I have numerous qualifications.
I have worked in industry.
I have tried to teach people.
People wanted me to work.
I have done mostly what they asked.
But it is now time for me to be me.
I will be retiring after this book.

No More Money

I gave you everything for years.
I have nothing left to give.
You took it all and burned me.
But now I am tired.
I am old and worn out.
I kept you going for a long time.
I did everything you ever wanted.
It is now time to forget.
It is now time to forgive.
It is now time to heal.

So Sorry

I am so sorry I cannot do anything.
I know we all feel pain.
But I am one of the people as well.
It has been a long mental illness.
But I will always need medication.
That is my reality.
Think yourself lucky you are not me.

ANDREW ALDRED

Love Lessons

Have your final love lesson.
You go your way, and I will go mine
You take the high road, and I will take the low road.
We are all going to be in the ground eventually.
Don't play with witchcraft and tarot cards.
Don't ever play games with anyone.
Sooner or later, nobody will play with you.
And we can all get our real heads on again.

Party People

We watch celebrities on TV having a party.
Disabled kids doing fantastic things.
People with great haircuts playing football.
Celebrities playing celebrity games.
Gangsters and other people making movies.
Its all celebrity this and celebrity that
I watch the wrestling on my phone.
I hardly ever watch telly these days.
My idea of a party is not playing charades.
It is not showing off in front of my family.
I want to have a beer and listen to music.
Everybody is busy being a celebrity.
I am busy being me in my house.
Well fuck all you party people.
I can have a beer and listen to music by myself.

Hope Your Happy

Well, my brother still wants to know me.
But I do not really want to know anyone else.
I never wanted children of my own.
I did not like the childhood I had.
I have been reduced to very little.
People have cut me down to size.
You want me to do everything with no reward.
Well, hey, have a go yourselves.
I guess you will all be getting on.
If you are walking down the street
You can say hello, but I might ignore you.
I guess I have written these books for myself.
Because it kept me occupied
Hope you're all happy. Goodbye

Moving Out

I guess I cannot wait to leave.
This town does not want me anymore.
People are knocking on my door at night.
Sometimes they are coming in and abusing me.
I am well aware the Asians want my home.
But I am too old to work for them.
I am not possessed by the devil.
Just my ex-girlfriend and the community
I know I have to leave this town as soon as possible.
That is if I want to live much longer.

Moving Out Part 2

I have bought everything I need on the internet.
I am trading in my car for a van.
I am selling my house to We Buy Any House
I am going to take what I can and get out.
It is all too much and always has been.
This time I know what is going on.
And everybody really has got me beat.
It is goodbye to Bolton. I am leaving.
I have a one-bedroom flat somewhere else.
I will take what I can and leave the rest.
Everyone has really led me up the garden path.
It is time I opened my eyes to what they are telling me.

Give You Your Due

I always said I wanted you to have a house.
And I guess its going to have to be our parents.
I have enough money and I will let you have my share.
In order to start a new life with your fiancée
It is what my parents wanted in retrospect.
I do not want a Cain and Abel situation.
I will take second best yet again.
At least you have been there for me.
And I might have been difficult for you.
But do not think I have had an easy time.
I will be coming up shortly and re-rooting myself.
I should have done this thirty years ago.

The Jihad in Bolton

Bolton is a mostly Muslim town.
It is half Asian and half white.
Those with jobs get on.
Those without do not
If you are in an Asian area
They want you to work for them.
And if you are in a white area
It is usually the same.
They pick on the ill and the isolated.
There is not enough money for them.
This society is so brutal.
They think I am the devil.
But they really do not know any better

Religion

Religion is the cause of many wars.
And the cause of a lot of hatred
The black people hate the whites.
The Asians think they are superior.
They exploit any weakness in the system.
They really hit you where it hurts.
Religion, sexuality, creed and colour
They are the things that keep people divided.
I always believed in one world.
But nowadays it is an outdated idea.
And everyone is busy killing each other.

Said Enough

You know I really should not have opened my mouth.
And told you what is going on in the world today.
But I had to do it to make myself sane.
It is as if I had suddenly woken up to a lot of things.
And yes, I have been awake for days.
But I am not going crazy. I am getting out.
I hope you have enjoyed my story.
And that one day you have one of your own.

No Money

I would move somewhere else.
If I had anyone to support me
If I could afford a decent house
If my past did not follow me around
I do not like the people next door.
And they have upset me in a nasty way.
But I have lived with murderers and rapists.
In her majesty's prisons and mental hospitals
And I do not want to live on the street.
So, I paid the estate agents off.
And reclaimed my house as my own.
And I will live here and face the music.
My girlfriend still wants to know me.
She loves me and I am still some use.
There is no money to move out of Farnworth.

Lifetime Love

Some people fall in love multiple times.
And some people sort things out.
With the partner they have got and intend to keep
I fall into the latter category.
I was not getting on with my girlfriend.
I had some trouble in the neighbourhood.
But I have complained to the police.
I have got in touch with mental health services.
And it had better get sorted out.
Jane is the only girl I have ever loved.
I am a similar age with similar disabilities.
We suit each other very well in some ways.
And when I bothered to ring her
She picked up the phone and talked to me.
We have mended our relationship.
I love her and I know she loves me.
And if anything re-affirms that it is recent events
I will never get another lifetime love.
So, I had better stick with this one.

Starlets

They are all over the internet.
Peddling their wares to everyone
They are on late night TV.
You can talk to them if you want.
A few of them were interested in me.
But I prefer the woman I have got.
I am too old to be all about sex.
I need somebody who can cook.
Somebody to give me cuddles and kisses.
Someone who will not take all my money.
I was never the life and soul of the party.
Always the quiet onlooker in a corner
I am not very much, and I know it.
And I just want to be who I am.
Because that is what suits me
Starlets are for the younger men.
And those with plenty of money
I am flattered they took an interest.
But I am no longer on the internet.
All I want is the life I have.

Sectarianist

Life is so sectarianist these days.
Everyone is divided in every way.
It is not just what is going on in Palestine.
Or the war in Ukraine or anywhere else
You have got to fit in a box to satisfy people.
Everybody wants to pigeonhole you.
You have to conform to some sort of sexuality.
Some form of race and religion
You have to be rich, poor or destitute.
You have to fly the party flag.
But I am none of these things.
I follow my own rules and always will.
The rest of the world can divide itself up.
And argue and fight over stupid things.
But I will be doing my best to get on.
They can call me mentally ill if they want.
And I will always need to take the tablets.
I am just a common ex-soldier.
I never made it to being any rank
You can have your sectarianist society.
But I will trade it in for my own freedom.

Hope is All We Have

When things are going badly for everyone
When you have taken as much as you can stand
You know you can never give up.
Because eventually you will be dead anyway
There is always the hope that things will be sorted out.
That things will get better for everyone.
And that will include yourself and your family.
If you want to build a better society
We all need to listen to each other.
I am getting on in years, but I do care.
I want a better society for everyone.
That is why I have expressed my point of view.
That is why I am appealing to you.
To find better ways of doing things
To improve what is already there.
And to leave a man that is old and tired alone.
To live the last years of his life in peace
I will leave it there. Hope is all we have.